LET THE INTERCESSORS ARISE!

Entering The Throne of Grace

(The Heart of An Intercessor)

"And he saw that there was no man, and wondered that there was no intercessor: therefore his arm brought salvation unto him; and his righteousness, it sustained him (Isaiah 59:16 KJV)."

Dr. Tonya Stewart

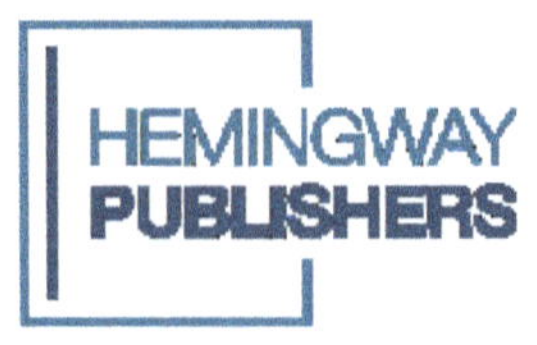
HEMINGWAY
PUBLISHERS

GRATITUDE AND THANKSGIVING

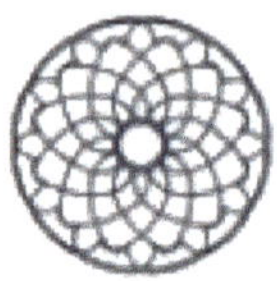

Prayer can change any situation. Reflecting on memories of growing up reminds me today of how thankful I am that God put me on somebody's heart to pray for me. The songwriter said, "Somebody prayed for me had me on their mind took the time to pray for me" "I am so glad they prayed for me (Dorthy Norwood)."

Thank you, Jesus, for praying for me and being my advocate when Satan wanted to sift me as wheat. Thank You Daddy (Pastor Alex Griffin) and Momma (Georgia Griffin), for praying for me always as my parents. Thank you (Pastor Shirley Deavens) for allowing me to grow from a prayer warrior into an intercessor. Thank you for every opportunity to pray and stand in the gap for the people who attended Abundant Life Encounter sessions. Thank you to all the leaders who prayed and stood in the gap for me. Thank you, babe (Bishop Kenneth Stewart), for the intercessory prayer time when we intercede for each other and those on our prayer list every day. Thank you, Kenny G and Kayla Carla (dog), for all your prayers. I'm so grateful someone taught me how to pray and stand in the gap for others as an intercessor.

Also, we would like to thank our Overseer, Bishop Priestess, and Lady Thomas & Hiers of God for your prayers. Apostle Brian Edwards, thank you for obeying and prophesying what thus saith the Lord by reminding me to finish a book God gave me years ago. Let the Intercessor Arise!

INTRODUCTION

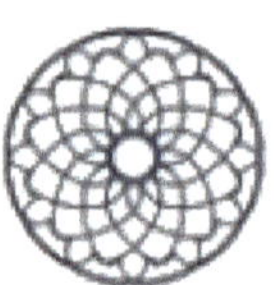

Entering the Throne of Grace, the heart of the intercessor is one who has a burning desire to pray for the needs and requests of others. God is seeking and calling Intercessors to stand in the gap for nations, firemen, police officers, marriages, families, and any situations where they need to Arise. The Holy Spirit is the one who prompts the intercessors to arise to pray at different times of the day.

In fact, as one reads the Bible, they can find in the Old and New Testament men and women of God who had the privilege and opportunity to plead, stand in the gap, cry out, and pray to God for mercy and grace. Before God made his final decision to pass judgment regarding sinful situations, he looked for an intercessor.

A remarkable example can be found in the book of Ezekiel, where God was looking for an intercessor who would stand in the gap and pray for the needs of others. Why? Intercessors are people who engage the enemy on the battlefield before any other ministry can truly take place. Once intercessory prayer goes forth, it opens the door for God to change and intervene in the situations supernaturally. Where there is no intercessor, judgment lies at the door. "So, I sought for a man among them who would make a wall, and stand in the gap before, me on behalf of the land that I should not destroy it, but I found no one (Ezekiel 22:30 KJV)." Then God sent Ezekiel to prophesy against the sin of Jerusalem, declaring He had no choice but to judge the land. Then God gives a picture of an intercessor as one who stands in a hole in a wall made for the enemy to keep him out. Therefore, let the Intercessors rise to their appointed prayer position!

CONTENTS

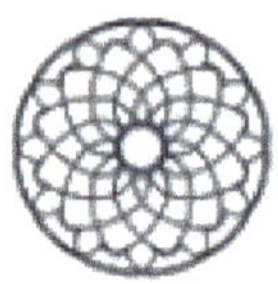

BLANK PAGE INTENTIONALLY

THE CHAMBER ROOM EXPERIENCE

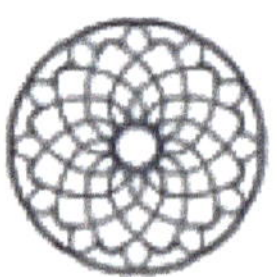

The Chamber-room experience is a specially designed place where believers meet God to fellowship and pray in His presence. Often, leaders, believers, and intercessors create a special prayer chamber room to start their day by praying, reading the Word, worshiping, and listening to praise music. This special prayer chamber room is referred to as the Secret Place of the Most-High God (Psalms 91:1), the Throne of Grace (Hebrews 4:16), or the Holy of Holies (Hebrews 9:11). The Book of Matthew, it is mentioned as a prayer room by saying "but when you pray, go into your most private room, close the door, and pray to your Father who sees [what is done] in secret will reward you (Matthew 6:6 AMP)." Jesus explained to the disciples that their motives and prayer requests should be] from a sincere heart and not full of vain repetition.

As intercessors grow and develop their relationship with God through Jesus Christ, they learn to pray not only for themselves but also for others. "Now the Lord is a Spirit; and where the Spirit of the Lord is there is Liberty (2 Corinthians 3:17 AMP)." As believers pray and fellowship with the Lord, they can open doors to receive liberty from bondages, cares, strongholds, and yokes in their lives while being in His presence.

When Intercessors are in the presence of the Lord, he reveals "the paths of life, the fullness of joy, and his right hand of pleasures forevermore (Psalm 16:11 AMP)." David gives insight into how God takes care of his people when they obey his instructions. The instructions from God provide direction for David on how to gain victory. Intercessors who listen and follow the direction of the Holy Spirit can receive insight and revelation on how to intercede for a particular problem, person, or place. As prayer and intercession go forth, give God access; he needs to provide divine intervention and divine turnaround regarding any situation. In fact, intercessors present and release all cares, concerns, and problems unto God so he can handle them. The heart of an Intercessor must remember to keep the right spirit, right motives, and proper attitude while praying, making their request private and public before the Father in the name of Jesus.

Intercessors who pray should come from a heart of repentance, humility, obedience, and love. Although "all the ways of a man are clean and innocent in his own eyes [and he may see nothing wrong with his actions], But the Lord weighs and examines the motives and intent [of the heart and knows the truth (Proverb 16:2 AMP)."

Therefore, the position of intercessors when they are in their personal Chamber Rooms praying and having an experience in the presence of the Lord can freely lay everything concerning their hearts and others on the Altar.

Intercessors can pray in a prostrated position at the Altar, in their prayer chamber on their faces, with humble knees (rusty), or sitting with their hearts open toward Heaven. This is the time to ask the Father, in the name of Jesus, to heal the land, people, and nation from the burdens of life. It is written in the Bible, "casting all your cares [all your anxieties, all your worries, and all your concerns, once and for all] on Him, for He cares about you [with deepest affection, and watches over you very carefully] (1 Peter 5:7 KJV)."

Intercessors who believe and continue to walk by faith can build a trusting and intimate relationship with God the Father through His Son, Jesus Christ, and the Holy Spirit every day in prayer. This type of intimacy fuels a burning desire for the intercessors to draw closer to the Lord in their hearts, minds, thoughts, and souls. This creates the right attitude for Intercessors who hunger and thirst for more of God's presence and His Spirit. David uses the image of a deer to illustrate how believers should long for the Lord. "As the deer pants [longingly] for the water brooks, so my [a]soul pants [longingly] for You, O God. My soul (my life, my inner self) thirsts for God, for the living God (Psalms 42:1-2 AMP)." Intercessors continue to thirst, and hunger for more God's Spirit will become satisfied and fill the empty places in their hearts. Intercessors Arise in prayer with clean hands, pure hearts, and a renewed right Spirit like David describes and requested from the Lord. He said, "Create in me a clean heart, O God, and renew a right spirit within me (Ps 51:10 KJV, Ps 24:1-10 KJV).

CHAPTER 2

ENCOUNTERS FACE TO FACE WITH GOD

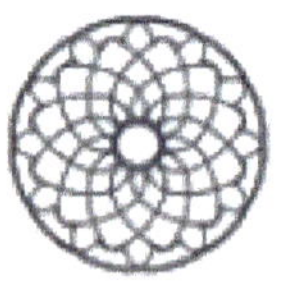

While intercessors are in the presence of the Lord, they can draw closer to real experiences and encounters with Him face to face. The Biblical stories illustrated below demonstrate how people can have face-to-face encounters with God and live.

Face To Face

Isaiah gives an example of how intercessors can have a burning desire and yearning to be in the presence of the Lord. He had a revelation from God on how to draw closer through a holy vision. "In the year that King Uzziah died, I saw [in a vision] the Lord sitting on a throne, high and exalted, with the train of His royal robe filling the [most holy part of the] temple. "Above Him, seraphim (heavenly beings) stood; each one had six wings: with two wings, he covered his face, with two wings he covered his feet, and with two wings he flew. "And one called out to another, saying, "Holy, Holy, Holy is the Lord of hosts; The whole earth is filled with His glory." "And the foundations of the thresholds trembled at the voice of him who called out, and the temple was filling with smoke." Then I said, "Woe is me! For I am ruined because I am a man of [ceremonially] unclean lips, and I live among a people of unclean lips.

"For my eyes have seen the King, the Lord of hosts." "Then one of the seraphim flew to me with a burning coal in his hand, which he had taken from the altar with tongs." "He touched my mouth with it and said, listen carefully, this has touched your lips; your wickedness [your sin, your injustice, your wrongdoing] is taken away and your sin atoned for and forgiven (Isaiah 6:1-7 AMP)."

This is a remarkable example of God manifesting his presence before his people through the Prophet Isaiah. Prophet Isaiah was given a vision of the Lord in the year King Uzziah died, signaling the end of an era. He saw the Lord seated on the throne high and lifted, and the train of his robe filled the temple.

Isaiah was given a difficult message, assignment, and mission from the Lord. Like everyone else who has a supernatural encounter with God, he felt unworthy to be there because of his sin. God, who is Holy, requires moral perfection. He purifies us from sin, cleanses our minds from our problems, enables us to worship, and then allows us to serve him.

The vision Isaiah witnessed was an encounter with the Lord face to face. As he listened to the praises of the angels, he recognized how unclean he was before the Lord. Then Isaiah by revelation from the Holy Spirit, realized how he did not measure up to God's standards and holiness. Isaiah began to totally submit to God as he confessed and acknowledged his sins of having unclean lips before God's presence and majesty. As a result, the angel put a burning coal on his lips, God purified him, and he was told his sins were forgiven.

God is releasing a message to all believers and intercessors today, urging them to come in His presence like Isaiah and lay their concerns, hurts, pain, disappointments, and whatever is holding them back from receiving healing or deliverance in their souls. Intercessors with a consistent prayer lifestyle must continue to fast, pray, practice humility, love, submit, surrender, and obedience, and have clean hands, pure hearts, and right motives in the presence of the Lord every day. This kind of attitude opens the opportunity for intercessors and believers to access the presence of the Lord and receive his blessing and righteousness. In Psalm 24:3 the passage begins by asking questions: "Who may ascend the mountain of the Lord? Who may stand in his holy place?" (Psalm 24:3-10 KJV). Even though everyone is God's creation or a born-again believer, but only certain ones are allowed to enter and stand in his Holy place.

Jacob Encounter Face to Face With God:
Genesis 32:24-34 AMP

The text begins with Jacob being left alone and wrestling with God until daybreak. When the man saw that He had not prevailed against Jacob, He touched his hip joint, dislocating it as they wrestled. The man said, "Let me go, for day is breaking."

But Jacob said, "I will not let you go unless you declare a blessing on me." The man asked Jacob, "What is your name?" Jacob spoke his name, and then the man said, "Your name shall no longer be Jacob, but Israel, for you have struggled with God and with men and have prevailed."

Jacob named the place Peniel (the face of God), saying, "For I have seen God face to face, yet my life has been spared (Genesis 24-34 AMP)." Jacob, now known as Israel, received a new name because he prevailed, gained victory, and received blessings from the Lord. This kind of attitude and persistence displayed by Jacob should always become the mindset and attitude of intercessors standing in the gap for others and not letting go until what is prayed for becomes a reality or they receive a release in their spirit that it is done.

Paul and Silas Encounter with the Presences of the Lord

Paul and Silas had an encounter with the Lord while they were fellowshipping with the father at Midnight, which is the end of one day and the beginning of another.

Paul described what happened during their time in jail, saying, "But at midnight, Paul and Silas were praying and singing hymns to God, and the prisoners were listening to them." "Suddenly there was a great earthquake so that the foundations of the prison were shaken' and immediately all the doors were opened, and everyone's chains were loosed during this time (Acts 17:25-26 KJV)."

Praying and signing was a way of life for Paul and Silas despite their current situation. Their songs of praise shifted the atmosphere, leading to the supernatural release of God's power and divine intervention. Paul and Sillas suddenly experienced a move of God because the doors were opened, and everyone's chains were loosed from the bondage that had them bonded.

God is seeking and looking for Intercessors and believers to keep the right Spirit and attitude during trials, tribulations, and the fiery tests in life. When Intercessors and believers Arise, pray, worship, and sing unto the Lord can witness the manifestation of God's presence, his power, and divine intervention during the test.

Paul's Intimate Relationship with Jesus Christ

Apostle Paul reveals and demonstrates how his desire to draw closer to knowing Jesus Christ, the Son of God not just through his intellectual knowledge of him. Instead, Paul was seeking relational knowledge of Christ's power on how to live day by day by the experience of being in Christ. "The "in Christ" We can do all things, I am God's workmanship created "in Christ," I am a new creature "in Christ," God has raised us up together, and made us sit together in heavenly places in Christ Jesus. Since all spiritual blessings are in Christ (Ephesians 1:3 AMP), "it is a faith relationship with him that allows believers to enjoy everything God offers in Christ." Therefore, as intercessors develop an intimate relationship with Christ, their faith continues to grow stronger under the guidance of the Holy Spirit.

Paul expressed his deep yearning and desire to know Jesus more. "And this, so that I may know Him [experientially, becoming more thoroughly acquainted with Him, understanding the remarkable wonders of His Person more completely] and [in that same way experience] the power of His resurrection [which overflows and is active in believers], and [that I may share] the fellowship of His sufferings, by being continually conformed [inwardly into His likeness even] to His death [dying as He did];(Philippians 3:10 AMP)," Paul reveals his yearning to know

Christ and live for him every day. This encourages believers and Intercessors to continue to draw closer and near to the Lord by following some of the suggestions listed below everyday:

1. Prayer.
2. Reading and Meditating on the Word of God.
3. Walking together with the Holy Spirit.
4. Following the Holy Spirit as he leads, guides, and fills us with fresh anointing of God's presence and spirit every day.
5. Practicing Agape Love.
6. Obedience.
7. Forgiveness.
8. Trust.
9. Faith.
10. Believe.
11. Love.
12. The Fruit of the Spirit.
13. Humility.
14. Submit.
15. Surrender.

Intercessors who live in the presence of God know how to keep the right Spirit during trials, tests, and tribulations. However, when they miss the mark, they run to the presence of God through the Name of Jesus to repent and ask God for forgiveness.

THE ROLE AND CHARACTER OF AN INTERCESSOR

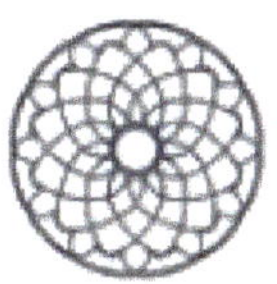

The role of intercessors involves petitioning God or praying on behalf of another person or group. Because the sinful nature of this world separates human beings from God. In both the Old and New Testaments. God looks for righteous individuals (intercessors) to go before Him and seek reconciliation between Him and His fallen creation. "For there is [only] one God, and [only] one Mediator between God and mankind, the Man Christ Jesus (1 Timothy 2:5 AMP)."

The sacrifices and prayers of the Old Testament priests were acts of intercession, which pointed forward to the work of Christ. In the Old Testament, it was the priest who was interceding and carrying out the role of an intercessor for the people. But in the New Testament, it is Jesus Christ who sits at the right hand of the Father, making intercession and acting as the High Priest (intercessor) for believers who come through him. "Therefore, He is able also to save forever (completely, perfectly, for eternity) those who come to God through Him, since He always lives to intercede and intervene on their behalf [with God] (Hebrews 7:25 APM)." Since Christ has a permanent priesthood position and he saves completely. The role of the believers and intercessors must come to God through Jesus Christ, and he intercedes as the mediator.

The Character and Attitude of An Intercessor

The Character of an intercessor displays the nature of God and the attitude of Christ. Listed below are some behaviors that should manifest through the heart of an intercessor.

A.   Courage of an intercessor means "laying hold of Jesus's heart, releasing His power through His Word and being confident that he will incline his ear to those who cry out to him (December 9, 2019, http://www.penhop.org)."

B.   Steadfastness as an intercessor is defined as asking God to intervene in the life of someone else. Intercessors develop an attitude to be diligent, focused, faithful, and determined. This happens when the intercessors "standing in the gap between them, future judgment, identifying with the sins of those from whom you are praying, asking God's forgiveness, and mercy on their behalf as if their sin was your own (https://www.kathrinewalden.com)."

C.   Endurance of an intercessor means to endure and never give up through difficult times while waiting patiently on the Lord to manifest divine intervention on someone else behalf. The intercessor is holding on, pleading, and praying to God through the blood and name of Jesus to give grace to the humble and mercy for the guilty before the judgment call.

D.   Boldness of an Intercessor has the tenacity to stand and risk our lives personally until God divinely intervenes in his will about the situation.

E.   Confidence of an intercessor means they have the assurance when they pray the Lord will hear and respond on behalf of someone else.

F.   Love of an intercessor means to demonstrate the selfless love of God by faith.

CHAPTER 4

THE HEART OF THE INTERCESSOR

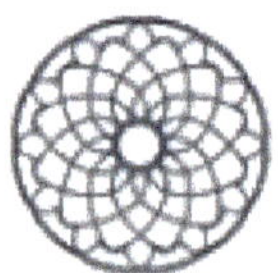

The heart of an intercessor is one who understands the meaning of praying without ceasing on behalf of others before the Lord. The heart of the intercessor stands in the gap as a mediator for people and those who do not pray for themselves. As intercessors, they have the heart to make requests, plead, risk, and fight for other people's needs. They are in the presence of the Lord, making intercession before the Father in the name of Jesus, seeking mercy instead of judgment, life over death, and blessing instead of curses. The heart of an intercessor has a burning desire to pray for God's people. They will arise when the Holy Spirit (quicken the intercessors) to pray for a particular person, place, or situation regardless of the time. The heart of an intercessor is ready to take risks and sacrifices to obtain mercy, whether on behalf of a loved one or a stranger. Where are the intercessors today? Let Them Arise! Sometimes, things are happening in many areas worldwide, and intercessors need to be awakened by the Holy Spirit to pray and intercede for these situations listed below:

1. Child or children.
2. Marriages.
3. All schools.
4. Hospitals.
5. Court room.
6. Churches.
7. Nursing Homes.
8. Mental Institutions.
9. Financial Organization.
10. President.
11. Single parents.
12. Israel.
13. Wars.

These are some of the major areas God needs an Intercessor to Arise and plead the blood of Jesus and stand in the gap for these people, places, and things.

Intercessors operate in faith, led and empowered by the Holy Ghost to speak the Word of God so he can intervene and turn situations around. "The eyes of the Lord are on the righteous, and his ears are attentive to their cry; the prayers of the righteous avail much (Psalms 34:15 KJV)." Let the Intercessors arise!

THE INTERCESSORS OF THE OLD TESTAMENT

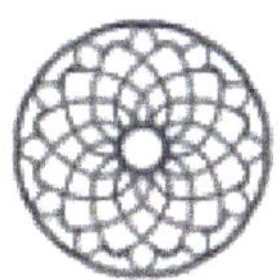

Isiaha the Prophet is the watchman who prays Prophetically as an Intercessor for Israel. "I have posted watchmen on your walls, Jerusalem; they will never be silent day or night. You who call on the Lord, give yourselves no rest, and give him no rest till he establishes Jerusalem and makes her the praise of the earth or instance: (Isaiah 62:6 KJV)."

In the Old and New Testaments, God used intercessors to stand in the gap. As we look around the world, problems are on the rise. Today, there are shootings in our schools and churches, and abuse is prevalent worldwide. This is why believers need to become intercessors, interceding and standing in the gap on behalf of each other. James mentions that we should pray for one another as believers. "Confess your faults one to another, and pray one for another, that ye may be healed. The effectual fervent prayer of a righteous man availeth much (James 5:16 KJV)." Let the Intercessors Arise! Arise means get or stand up. God is looking and seeking for intercessors to stand and intercede for others. Illustrated below are different stories in the Bible where God used leaders and prophets to pray and intercede for the people who sinned, rebelled, and disobeyed God's commandments.

Ezekiel 22:30

Israel's sins were for the shed blood, living immorally, disobedience, and rebellious ways. "So, I sought for a man among them who would make a wall and stand in the gap before me on behalf of the land, that I should not destroy it; but I found no one (Ezekiel 22:30)." This was a sad day in Israel history when God asked Ezekiel to with prophesying against the sins of Jerusalem, stating that He had no choice but to judge the land. This judgment could have been prevented if even one intercessor had pleaded on behalf of the land.

The wall referenced here is not built of stones but of faithful individuals united in their efforts to resist evil. This wall had fallen into disrepair because there was no leader to guide the people back to God. What the people truly needed was spiritual reconstruction by applying the Word of God and His principles, not religious rituals or messages based on their opinions. The people needed to apply and live by the word of God, then they would now how to join in together with other people by standing in the gap to make a difference in the world.

Abraham Genisis 18:20-33

Before God brings judgment upon Sodom and Gomorrah, Abraham is the intercessor who pleads on behalf of the righteous people who might be living in Sodom and Gomorrah. After all, Abraham negotiates with God regarding the two cities where Lot, his nephew and his family were staying. Notice Abraham was praying for cities more than individual people. He was praying for justice in the cities, salvation, and peace. So, Abraham starts off by asking God what could happen if he found 50 people living righteous. Would he destroy the two cities? Abraham pleads with God all the way down to 10 people. But God's judgment was passed upon Sodom and Gomorrah for their wickedness, idolatry, pride, and sexual perversion. However, God remembers Lot for the sake of Abraham.

Moses Number 14:17-23

Moses is interceding as an intercessor who stands in the gap on behalf of the children of Israel, pleading with God to forgive them. As an intercessor, Moses was one among all the people who were honest with total integrity, a deeper concern, and compassion for others with a pure heart, and clean hands. The Israelites had rejected God 10 times 10 by lacking trust during the time they were crossing over the Red Sea; they were murmuring and complaining about the bitter water at Marah and failed to trust God to enter the promised land. Because of the Israelites' rebellion, hard hearts, unbelief, double-mindedness, and disobedience, God's judgment came in the form the people feared the most. The people were afraid of dying in the desert, so God punished and passed judgment on the children of Israel by making them wander in the desert until they died.

Hezekiah 2 Chronicles 30:18-20

Hezekiah was a man who stood in the gap for the people who sinned and disobeyed the laws of God to serve other Gods and idols. "For a multitude of people, many from Ephraim, Manasseh, Issachar, and Zebulun, had not cleansed themselves, yet they ate the Passover contrary to what was written." "But Hezekiah prayed for them, saying, the good Lord pardon everyone." "Who the Lord God of his fathers, though he is not cleansed according to the purification of the sanctuary" "And the Lord hearkened to Hezekiah and healed the people (2 Chronicles30:18-20 KJV). Hezekiah prayed for them, asking God to observe the desires of their hearts. In response, God healed the people and their relationship with him. Genuinely seeking after God is more important than adherence to ritual.

Queen Esther 4:1-17

The story about Queen Esther as an Intercessor on assignment was revealed when

Mordecai would not bow before Haman to pay homage; he became full of wrath. Then Haman pursued his plot to kill Mordecai and destroy the Jewish nation. Queen Esther agreed to intervene with the Jewish community by prayer and fasting for protection on their behalf. As a result, God moved supernaturally for his people because of their prayers and fasting so the Jewish race would not be destroyed. This story can inspire intercessors today on how to stand on the Word of God by faith together and in unity. Therefore, the will of God is established on the earth through believers and intercessors arising and praying.

Jeremiah 11:14

Jeremiah showed compassion and empathy for the people by standing and interceding for their sins, disobedience, and idolatry. Since the children of Israel refuse to listen or obey the instruction of the Lord he sent by the Prophet so, God asked him not to "pray for this people: or lift up a cry or prayer for them; for I will not hear them in the time that they cry out to me become of their trouble (Jeremiah 11:14 KJV)." God decided to pass judgment instead of mercy upon the people. A lesson learned from Prophet Jeremiah is that when believers do not obey, judgment lies at the door even though an intercessor is on their watch. God has the final say!

Daniel 9:24

Daniel was a prayer warrior and intercessor who stood in the gap three times a day toward the East before the Lord, praying and interceding on behalf of the people's sins. "Then I set my face toward the Lord God to make request by prayer and supplication, with fasting, sackcloth, and ashes" (Daniel 9:3 KJV)." "Daniel said,

"And I prayed to the Lord my God, and made confession, and said, "O Lord, great and awesome God, who keeps His covenant and mercy with those who love him, and with those who keep his commandments (Daniel 9:4 KJV)." This is a prayer of repentance for Israel's sinfulness and a prayer of confidence. Even though God was about to overthrow the Babylonians and allow the Jews to return to their homeland to rebuild, Daniel confessed that Israel had departed from the Word of God, ignored the prophets of God, and despised the Lord. Therefore, God brought judgment and released a curse for the violation.

Nehemiah 1:11

Nehemiah was an intercessor who boldly stood in the gap for the people. As a leader, he was able to rebuild the broken walls in Jerusalem. "O Lord, please hear my prayer!" "Listen to the prayers of those of us who delight in honoring you." "Please grant me success today by making the king favorable to me. "Put it into his heart to be kind to me (Nehemiah 1:11 KJV)."

He asked God to look at him and listen to him as he prayed on behalf of Israel. His words were designed to encourage God not to turn his ears from or close his eyes to the children of Israel. Since they sinned against the Lord and disobeyed his commandments, Nehemiah then confessed the sins of his Father's house, nationally and personally. After Nehemiah confessed his sins and the sins of the people, he reminded God of his covenant and promise to Israel. Therefore, Nehemiah continues to plead on behalf of Israel, so the Lord would not scatter them among the nation but return the people to a place where God established his name.

Elijah 1 King 18:37-38

Elijah intercedes on behalf of the people as the intercessor when he asks God to reveal himself to the people by giving them a divine intervention. "Hear me, O Lord, hear me, that this people may know that you are the Lord God, and that you have turned their hearts back to you again (1 Kings 18:37 KJV)." Elijah's' prayer to the Lord would demonstrate clearly to the people that He alone is the living God. "Then the fire of the Lord fell and consumed the burnt sacrifice, and the wood and the stones, and the dust, and it licked up the water that was in the trench (1 Kings 18:38 KJV)." Then Elijah prayed for revival on behalf of God's people.

Ezra 9:5-14

Ezra is interceding as an intercessor for the children of Israel. He said, "At the evening sacrifice I arose from my fasting, and having torn my garment and my robe, I fell on my knees and spread out my hands to the Lord my God (Ezra 9:5 KJV)." Ezra discovered that the people had broken their covenant with God by marrying unbelievers and pagan wives. God specifically forbade them to marry unbelievers because he did not want his holy people to mix their seed with people who worship demons and practice abomination. God did not abandon the children of Israel, but he extended mercy. "For we were slaves. Yet our God did not forsake us in our bondage; but he extended mercy to us in the sight of the kings of Persia, to revive us, to repair the house of our God, to rebuild its ruins, and to give us a wall in Judah and Jerusalem (Ezra 9: 9 KJV)."

Prophet Anna Luke 2:37

Anna served in the house of God as a prophetess who interceded for the people of God. "This woman Anna was an eighty-four year old widow, who did not depart from the temple, but served God with fasting and prayers night and day (Luke 2:37 KJV)." Anna's work as a prophetess in the temple court suggests that she addressed all who would listen to her. A prophet's main role was to speak for God by proclaiming his truth.

The Old Testament Intercessors made sacrifices unto the Lord through a priest who prayed and made intercession on the people's behalf when they sinned and disobeyed God's commandments.

CHAPTER 6

NEW TESTAMENT INTERCESSORS

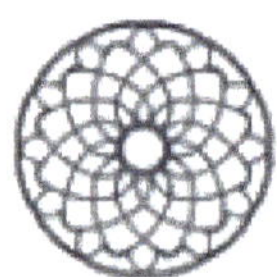

The Bible is divided into two major sections: the Old and New Testament. Apostle Paul declared, "For until this day the same veil remains unlifted in the reading of the Old Testament because the veil is taken away in Christ (2 Cor 3:14 KJV)." After reviewing how intercessors of the Old Testament were chosen leaders and prophets. Still, the New Testament Jesus is and continues to be the High Priest.

Intercession and Intercessory prayer is the act of praying to God on behalf of others by asking him to release divine intervention and turn around. This happens when God sends angels to help people, places, and situations when they arise. Believers are called to develop a relationship with God through Jesus Christ. Then, answer the call to become a Christ-centered intercessor who stands in the gap, interceding for the will of God to be done in the lives of the people.

Illustrated below are remarkable stories that demonstrate the heart of New Testament intercessors.

<u>Stephen Acts 7:59- 60</u>

While they were stoning him, Stephen prayed, "Lord Jesus, receive my spirit (Acts 7:59 KJV)." Stephen's assignment was complete, and he was ushered into the presence of Jesus. However, before he closed his eyes, Stephen stood in the gap for those who stoned him to death as he looked to heaven. "Then he fell on his knees and cried out, "Lord, do not hold this sin against them." When he had said this, he fell asleep (Acts 7:60 KJV)." He asks God to forgive his murderers and show them mercy. Because the accusers did not know what they did, which were words like Jesus spoke when he died on the cross. This kind of response comes from the Holy Spirit to help Stephen and believers to show love and mercy to their enemies.

LOVING OUR NEIGHBOR AS OURSELVES

When a person is offended by another person or group should practice forgiveness. The world says forgive but don't forget about what they did to you. Peter asked Jesus a question: how often shall my brother sin against me, and I forgive him? Jesus responds by saying up to seven times," Jesus said to him "I do not say to you, up to seven times, but up to seventy times seven (Matthew 18:21-22 KJV)."

Believers must turn the check when they are mishandled, used, and abused by other people. Mathew tells believers, "Do not treat evil with evil, but rather with love." It also says that if someone slaps you on your right cheek, you should turn the other cheek to them (Matthew 5:38-42 AMP)." You have heard that it was said, "You shall love your neighbor (fellow man) and hate your enemy." 44 But I say to you, [a]love [that is, unselfishly seek the best or higher good for] your enemies and pray for those who persecute you (Mathew 5:43-44 AMP)." Believers forgive so they may be forgiven, or the Father will not forgive the one who is offended or unforgiving.

God is love, and when believers overcome evil with good demonstrate the true love of God. Therefore, believers and intercessors should intercede for one another. So, hearts will not grow cold or bitter during the fiery trials of life. When Intercessors arose in the Old and New Testaments happened during times the people were practicing disobedience, rebellion, and idolatry. The Intercessor who rose pleaded for mercy in the Old and grace in the New Testament. "For the law was given through Moses: grace and truth came through Jesus Christ (John 1:17 KJV)."

In fact, mercy means "the aspect of God's love that causes Him to help the pity and show compassion and kindness, just as grace is the aspect of His love that moves Him to forgive sins and guilt (dictionary bible pg. 697)." The heart of intercessors cries out and stands in the gap for others at the Altar and in their Chamber room for mercy and grace. "Finally, because God is merciful, he expects His children to practice being merciful (James 1:27 KJV and Matthew 5:7 KJV)."

Jesus, The Advocate, High Priest, and Intercessor

Jesus the Advocate

Jesus is the one who makes intercession for every believer like an Advocate. He sits at the right side of God interceding for us all the time. An advocate is defined as "one who is called to our side, one who pleads another's cause, who helps another by defending, or comforting him (Thomas Nelson, 1897)." Jesus pleads on behalf of the believers for grace and mercy in the court room of heaven to the Father.

John reveals how Jesus speaks to the Father about his people. "My little children (believers, dear ones), I am writing you these things so that you will not sin and violate God's law. And if anyone sins, we have an Advocate [who will intercede for us] with the Father: Jesus Christ the righteous [the upright, the just One, who conforms to the Father's will in every way—purpose, thought, and action] (1: John 2:1AMP)." However, John's purpose is to keep his readers from sinning. Even though he knows at the same time they will sin. In God's grace, he restored sinning Christians, but he appointed Jesus as the advocate to plead on the case of the sinners.

<u>*A remarkable example: Jesus, the Advocate in the courtroom*</u>

When Satan, the accuser of the brothering, is lurking, going to and forth, seeking whom he can devour by making accusations against believers. Satan accuses by saying that believers do not qualify for the blessing from the Father. However, Jesus the Advocate says not guilty; it has been paid in full by the blood of the Lamb.

<u>*Jesus, The High Priest*</u>

In the Old Testament, High Priests were mediators between God and his human creation. In fact, their primary assignment was to offer sacrifices and gifts unto God to atone for the sins of the people. Jesus the High Priest according to Hebrews, states, "Therefore, it was essential that he had to be made like His brothers (mankind) in every respect, so that he might[by experience] become a merciful and faithful High Priest in things related to God, to make atonement (propitiation) for the people's sins [thereby wiping away the sin, satisfying divine justice, and providing a way of reconciliation between God and mankind(Hebrews 2:17 AMP)." Jesus testifies to every believer and Intercessor he has walked in their shoes. Jesus Christ experienced the same pain, frustrations, temptations, and trials believers and intercessors face today, but sin not. He understands since he had to go through them himself. The

High Priest must be one with the people in order to represent them. Therefore, Jesus had to become a man to be an effective High Priest. "The Word became flesh and made his dwelling among us, and we have seen his glory, glory as of the only Son from the Father, full of grace and truth (John 1:14 KJV)."

On the contrary, Jesus the High Priest in the New Testament "since then we have a great high priest who has passed through the heavens, Jesus, the Son of God, let us hold fast our confession." "For we do not have a high priest who is unable to sympathize with our weaknesses, but one who in every respect has been tempted as we are, yet without sin (Hebrews 4:14 KJV)." No matter what each believer or Intercessor struggles with, Jesus can identify with the problems, sins, heartaches, and pains without sinning. He wants to give believers and Intercessors the same overcoming power through the Holy Spirit to resist sin and be more than conquerors.

Just like Jesus prayed and interceded for Peter, "and the Lord said, Simon, Simon, behold, Satan hath desired to have you, that he may sift you as wheat: "But I have prayed for thee, that thy faith fail not: and when thou art converted, strengthen thy brethren (Luke 22:31-32 KJV)." Jesus interceded that Peter's faith would not fail in the midst of being tested and tried through his trials.

Jesus: The Intercessor

Jesus, the Intercessor between God and man. "Who is the one who condemns us? Christ Jesus is the One who died [to pay our penalty], and more than that, who was raised [from the dead], and who is at the right hand of God interceding [with the Father] for us (Romans 8:34 AMP)." Jesus the Intercessor is positioned at the right hand of God, standing in the gap and pleading on our behalf. Since Christ had fully justified us and is presently interceding for us, then no one can possibly condemn believers since he has already paid the price and penalty for sin.

CHAPTER 7

THE DIVINE INTERVENTION

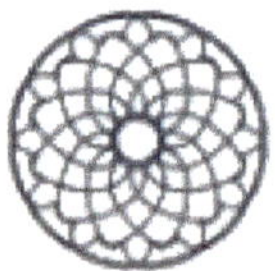

Divine interventions happen when intercessors and believers pray to God on behalf of someone, thing, or place. In fact, divine intervention invites God's presence or sends Angels to turn around situations, problems, and issues that arise. Divine intervention, according to "Webster's Dictionary" "is an event that happens when God becomes actively involved in changing some situation in human affairs(www.websterdictionary.org)." When, God Intervenes in the lives of his people, he seeks to bring adjustment, change, and turn things around. So, Intercessors intercede on behalf of others, praying the word of God. Why? God hastened to perform his word so divine intervention is released on their behalf. The stories listed here in the Bible reveal how God manifested his divine intervention when someone is in trouble and needs an intercessor to arise and pray.

Peter Acts 12:5-17

The text states Herod had killed James and now planned to kill Peter after the Passover. Peter was captured and kept in Prison, but constant prayer was offered to God for him by the Church (intercessory prayer). The church's first response was on rusty knees and offered up consent prayer to God on Peter's Behalf. "So, Peter was kept in prison, but the church was earnestly praying to God for him (Acts 12:5 AMP)." These constant and persevering prayers moved the hand and heart of God, and Peter was miraculously freed from jail by an Angel. When intercessors come together and pray, God can cause a divine turn around by sending Angels to intervene in any situation.

Moses Burning Bush Face to Face Exodus 3:2 AMP

Mose's divine encounter with God in the form of a burning bush was the turning point in his life after 40 years of being behind the mountain. "The [a]Angel of the Lord appeared to him in a blazing flame of fire from the midst of a bush; and he looked, and behold, the bush was on fire, yet it was not consumed (Exodus 3:2 AMP)." This was one of the significant turning points for Moses. The divine intervention convinced Moses to answer the call of God on his life. When was the last time you prayed for God to release divine intervention? God does everything by His Spirit. He wants to manifest His presence by shifting the atmosphere. When believers and intercessors decree, the Word of God changes situations.

1. Divine Turn Around.
2. Divine Alignment.
3. Divine Manifestation.
4. Divine Demonstration.
5. Divine Release.
6. Divine Breakthrough.
7. Divine Timing of God.
8. Divine Favor.
9. Divine Relationships.
10. Divine Strategies.
11. Divine Impartation.
12. Divine Health.

Believers are called to become intercessors, and the Holy Spirit lives in us, and He intercedes for us according to the will of God. "But the [a]Helper (Comforter, Advocate, Intercessor—Counselor, Strengthener, Standby), the Holy Spirit, whom the Father will send in My name [in My place, to represent Me and act on My behalf], He will teach you all things. "And He will help you remember everything that I have told you (John 14:26 AMP)." John introduces the Holy Spirit's role in the life of believers. He mentions how the Holy Spirit enables believers to understand the word of God and helps each of them live by the truth. Without the Holy Spirit, believers could not receive the things of the Spirit of God.

In fact, Intercessors and believers face situations, problems, and difficulties they cannot understand and do not see how to work through them. This is the time to ask the Holy Spirit of God inside of us to help us in our human limitations and weaknesses by interceding for us to God the Father. However, the Holy Spirit can speak through the believers in a Heavenly language. The book of Jude says, "But you beloved, build yourselves up in your most holy faith, pay in the Holy Ghost (Jude 1:20 KJV)." This allows the Holy Spirit to transcend our human intellect to speak on our behalf to the Father.

In the same way the Spirit [comes to us and] helps us in our weakness. "We do not know what prayer to offer or how to offer it as we should, but the Spirit Himself [knows our need and at the right time] intercedes on our behalf with sighs and groanings too deep for words. "And He who searches the hearts knows what the mind of the Spirit is, because the Spirit intercedes [before God] on behalf of [a]God's people in accordance with God's will (Romans 8:26-27 AMP)."

The Holy Spirit prays effective prayers when believers do not know how. At the same time, believers are groaning and sighing with loud cries and tears of the expressions from the heart and spirit in prayer. Then, intercessors are interceding by the Holy Spirit and making effective intercession before the Father in the throne of Grace.

CHAPTER 8

THE KINGDOM LANGUAGE OF AN INTERCESSOR

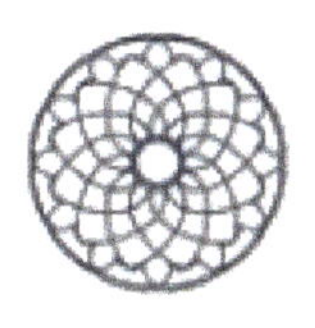

MATTHEW 18:18 AMP

Kingdom language is dynamic and essential for believers and intercessors to practice living and speaking every day. After all, language is how intercessors communicate with God when they pray. The language of the Kingdom of God says, "And the whole earth was of one language and one speech (Genesis 11:1 KJV)." When intercessors walk in the Authority of Jesus Christ has the keys to shift the atmosphere by speaking the Word of God.

When the intercessors arise and use their Kingdom language to bind the enemy, they lose the will and Word of God in the atmosphere over people, places, or things. Mathew explains the power of speaking the Word of God. "I assure you and most solemnly say to you, whatever you bind [forbid, declare to be improper and unlawful] on earth [a]shall have [already] been bound in heaven, and whatever you loose [permit, declare lawful] on earth [b]shall have [already] been loosed in heaven (Matthew 18:18 AMP)."

When intercessors decree, declare, and call forth the Word of God on behalf of others can counterattack the enemy in the Spirit realm through prayer and intercession. This will cancel, abort, stop, and prevent the hand of the enemy from carrying out the assignment against the believer. Intercessors remind God of his Word, which gives him access to manifest divine intervention and send Angels forth on assignment to turn the situation around. "So shall they fear the name of the Lord from the west and His glory from the rising of the sun. "When the enemy shall come in like a flood, the Spirit of the Lord shall lift up a standard against him (Isaiah 59:19 KJV)." The Lord is our defense and will drive the enemy back when he comes against the children of God.

Therefore, intercessors understand the fight is in the Spiritual realm and the results are manifested in the natural. "For we wrestle not against flesh and blood, but against principalities, against powers, against the rulers of the darkness of this world, against spiritual wickedness in high places (Ephesians 6:12 KJV)."

Intercessors and believers fight is spiritual and not physical, so when the fight happens believers and intercessors put on the Armor of God.

Jesus went forth in his Kingdom Authority, rebuking and casting out demons many times with sone-word syllable concepts. The words and kingdom language he spoke demonstrated the power and authority that manifest miracles, signs, and wonders. "For the Kingdom of God is not in word, but in power (1 Corinthians 4:20 KJV)." The scripture reveals how the supernature power of God was released through the words Jesus spoke when he healed, delivered, and set the captives free.

Listed are words that released the supernatural power of God to heal, deliver, and set the captive free.

1.   Abolish- "to end, cut, strike, through" (Isaiah 2:18, II Timothy 1:10 KJV).

2.   Beat down- "beat, bruise, strike, crush, breakdown, and dismay." (Exodus 34:13; Ps. 2:9, Jer. 28:4, Dan. 2:40 KJV).

3.   Cast Out- "to occupy by driving out the previous strongholds, bondages, tenants, to seize, to rob, to send away, to push away or down, and throughout. (Exodus. 34:24, Lev. 18:24, Matt. 12:28, Mark 6:13; Luke 6:13)."

4.   Confound - "to be ashamed, disappointed, be put to shame" (Ps. 35:4; Jer 17:18; Jer 50:2, Ps. 109:29 KJV).

5.   Destroy- "to end, to cease, destroy utterly, make clean, waste, tear down, beat down, break down to devour (Lev. 26:30; Ps. 5:6; Mark 1:24; Mathew 21:41; 1 John 3:8 KJV)."

6.   Contend- "to grant, to defend, rebuke" (Isa. 41:12; Isa. 49:25; Jude 9 KJV).

7.   Flight- "to consume, to battle, make war, overcome, prevail" (Exod. 14:14; Deut. 1:30; Josh. 10:25, Judg. 1:1; Ps 35:1; Heb.10:32; 1Tim:12 KJV)."

8.   Prevail- "to enclose, to hold back, shut up, stop, restrain, bind, and conquer"

(II Chron. 14:11; Ps 9:19; Isa. 42:13; Matt. 16:18 KJV).

9.   Smite- "strike, beat, cast forth, slay, defeat" (Num.25:17; Deut. 13:15; Jer. 43:11; Acts 7:24; Rev. 11:6, Josh. 7;3).

10.   Wrestle- "to struggle and grapple" (Gen. 30:8; 32:24; Eph. 6:12).

The sound of intercessor within the believer goes forth like a 911 in the presence of the Lord. Why? Because intercessors who call on the name of the Lord on someone's behalf are an emergency, and they need divine intervention to be released from the Lord. After all, the heart of the intercessors who stand in the gap prevents demonic attacks from happening to a loved one or stranger.

Therefore, Satan tries to make intercessors and believers walk in unbelief and doubt the promises of God. Faith looks to God, who keeps his promises, and hope helps believers and intercessors to look for things he promised his people. Hebrews says it is impossible for him to lie. "Therefore, we who have fled to him for refuge can have great confidence as we hold to the hope that lies before us." "This hope is a strong and trustworthy anchor for our souls." "It leads us through the curtain into God's inner sanctuary." "Jesus has already gone in there before us. He has become our eternal High Priest in the order of Melchizedek (Hebrews 6:18-20 KJV)."

When the Intercessors Arise will pray the prayer of faith, believing God for miracles, signs, and wonders in the lives of the people so they can receive the promises he has for them, God wants us to pray for others, so believers think beyond themselves and grow in compassion and a burning desire to pray for others. This pleases God when intercessors pray the will of God on the earth. John illustrated what our prayers smell like in the presence of the Lord. In fact, John said, "God compares prayers with a sweet-smelling incense that pleases him (Revelation 5:8 AMP)." Let the Intercessor Arise and pray in the name of Jesus and through the power of the blood!

Jesus has given believers and intercessors authority and keys to tread upon the enemy. Luke said, "Listen carefully: I have given you authority [the ability to exercise authority] over all the power of the enemy (Satan): and nothing will [in anyway] harm you (Luke 10:19AMP)." Therefore, Jesus has given intercessors and believers Kingdom authority to take dominion over the powers of darkness operating in people's lives, their homes, communities, and nations. However, Kingdom authority is manifested through praying in the name of Jesus. In fact, John says, "Whatever you ask in my name, I will do it so that the Father may be glorified in the Son (John 14:13 KJV)." Let The Intercessors Arise and pray!

REFERENCE

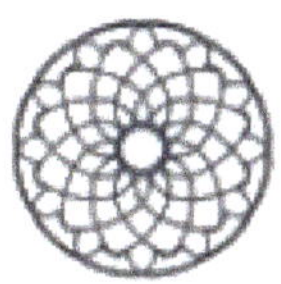

December 9, 2019, (http://www.penhop.org).

<u>https://www.kingjamesbibleonline.org</u>

<u>https://www.kathrinewalden.com</u>

M.G. Easton M.A., D.D., Illustrated Bible Dictionary, Third Edition, published by Thomas Nelson, 1897. Public Domain, copy freely.

https://www.websterdictionary.org

INTERCESSORY SCRIPTURES

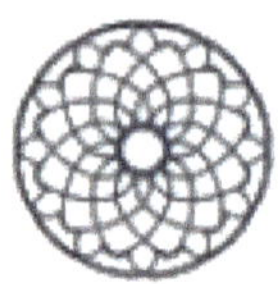

1 Timothy 2:1 - I exhort therefore, that, first of all, supplications, prayers, intercessions, and giving of thanks, be made for all men.

Matthew 18:19-20 - Again I say unto you, That if two of you shall agree on earth as touching anything that they shall ask, it shall be done for them of my Father which is in heaven. (Read More...)

Ephesians 6:18 - Praying always with all prayer and supplication in the Spirit and watching thereunto with all perseverance and supplication for all saints.

John 16:23-24 - And in that day ye shall ask me nothing. Verily, verily, I say unto you, Whatsoever ye shall ask the Father in my name, he will give it to you.

Jude 1:20 - But ye, beloved, building up yourselves on your most holy faith, praying in the Holy Ghost,

Job 42:10 - And the LORD turned the captivity of Job, when he prayed for his friends: also the LORD gave Job twice as much as he had before.

PRAYER FOR THE INTERCESSORS

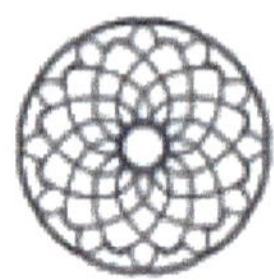

Father, in the name of Jesus, we come standing in the gap for the Intercessors who Arise every morning, noon, and evening, interceding on behalf of others. Father, we are asking, in the name of your Son, Jesus Christ, that you will renew their strength to keep obeying the voice of the Holy Spirit. Father give them grace and mercy to keep praying without ceasing. Father, in the name of Jesus, we ask you to fulfill every need for the intercessors who are reading this prayer. Father, through the power of the blood and the name of Jesus, we plead the blood over their families, marriages, children, fiancés, and everyone who concerns them. Father, in the name of Jesus, we pray you will reveal the revelations of dreams, vision, and knowledge of what you are doing in the earthly realm. We bind Satan and his demonic forces from hindering, blocking, distracting, and preventing the intercessors from moving forward every day to pray the Will of the Lord for the people of God. Father, we pray in the name of Jesus that you would protect the intercessors from hurt, harm, or danger by sending angels to surround them everywhere they go. Lord, we are asking you to release the spirit of wisdom, knowledge, understanding, and godly counsel upon them. Father the God of all comfort we are pleading for love, peace, sound mind, mercy, and grace for all intercessors worldwide. Father, we seal this prayer through the Spirit, blood, and name of Jesus.

OTHER BOOKS FOR
DR. TONYA K. STEWART

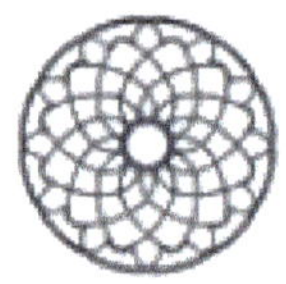

Livinglife690@yahoo.com

314-441-2771

<u>The Flame That Never Dies: Kindling the Flame Igniting the Fire Within</u>

There is a flame that never dies out. Its fire is sustained through an intimate relationship with the Holy Spirit. As believers when we stay connected to the fire our flame will never die out. Jesus lights the torch with the Holy Ghost Fire which enables us to live and walk in our destiny.

<u>From Desperation to Determination: How To Overcome the Challenges in Life and Win Like a Champion?</u>

As a believer in life, pursuing a purpose will face challenges. However, greater is he that is in me than he that is in the world. The same God who gave the assignment also has the strategies and how-to factors to win the battle! Champions are made every day because they learn to never give up in the middle of a test but hold on to God's unchanging hands. Every believer can become a Champion by developing a Christ-like Character and Eagle Mentality.

Unveiling The Hand of the Enemy

There are remarkable and phenomenal concepts used to expose the hand of the enemy in the Bible. When a believer is exposed to the truth can choose to do what is right or wrong based on the principles and standards of the Word of God. Decisions believers make in life determine if they will live in freedom or bondage. The choice is ours. After all, God did not make his creation robots. Once a person receives Jesus Christ as Lord and Savior no longer is he or she blind to the tactics of the enemy. God loves his children and has given us dominion, authority, and the Holy Ghost power over Satan through Jesus Christ.

I Am SAVED Now What? Growing and Maturing by Grace of God as a New Believer in Christ

I Am Saved Now What? It is a book that provides Principles and Standards on how to live a Christian Lifestyle in victory. I Am SAVED to know What? It will reveal how to factors to enhance, develop, and teach a babe in Christ how to grow in their relationship with the Father through Jesus Christ.

Living Life By Connecting the Dots Series 1 Birthing Out the Formative Stages of Life

Character Development produces ethical changes in the mindset which impacts moral behavior patterns and attitudes. Attributes valued and implemented produce self-discipline and obedience. Now for this very reason also, applying all diligence, in your faith supplies moral excellence, and in your moral excellence, knowledge (2 Peter 1:5 KJV)."

Living Life By Connecting The Dots, Series 2-3 Birthing Out the Finish Work of Christ Inside Out

Seeing A Vision That Can Happen in your Life Creates a positive mindset and assists in focusing on the goals that wait for each of us to accomplish. The Word of the Lord is utilized as spiritual components for each person who believers in Jesus Christ. God's power of the Holy Spirit is our helper to overcome and transform people's Character and Love.

Delivered by Truth Freed by Grace

Delivered by Truth Feed by Grace Reveals remarkable keys and principles to assist believers on how to break free individually and corporately from strongholds and bondages designed by Satan to trap Elohim's creation. However, believers can change what they believe once they have discovered the lies, they have received in their hearts. The choice to change will depend on our willingness to transform our mindset through the power of the Word of God and the leading of the Holy Spirit and fire. The truth we receive in our hearts comes to make us accessible when we uproot the wrong behavior patterns and implement the fruit of the Spirit.

Activating the Kingdom of God Through A Christ-like mindset

This happens when believers become born again. Then believers begin to walk in the Kingdom of God. As a new creation in Christ renewing their mind to think like Christ will transform the attitude to function and operate as sons and daughters in the King of God.

Food For Thought

Food For Thought gives a believer or person a place to put thoughts of inspiration and revelation revealed at a special time from the Lord. The moment it comes write down and reflect later as a Mindful Moment in life.

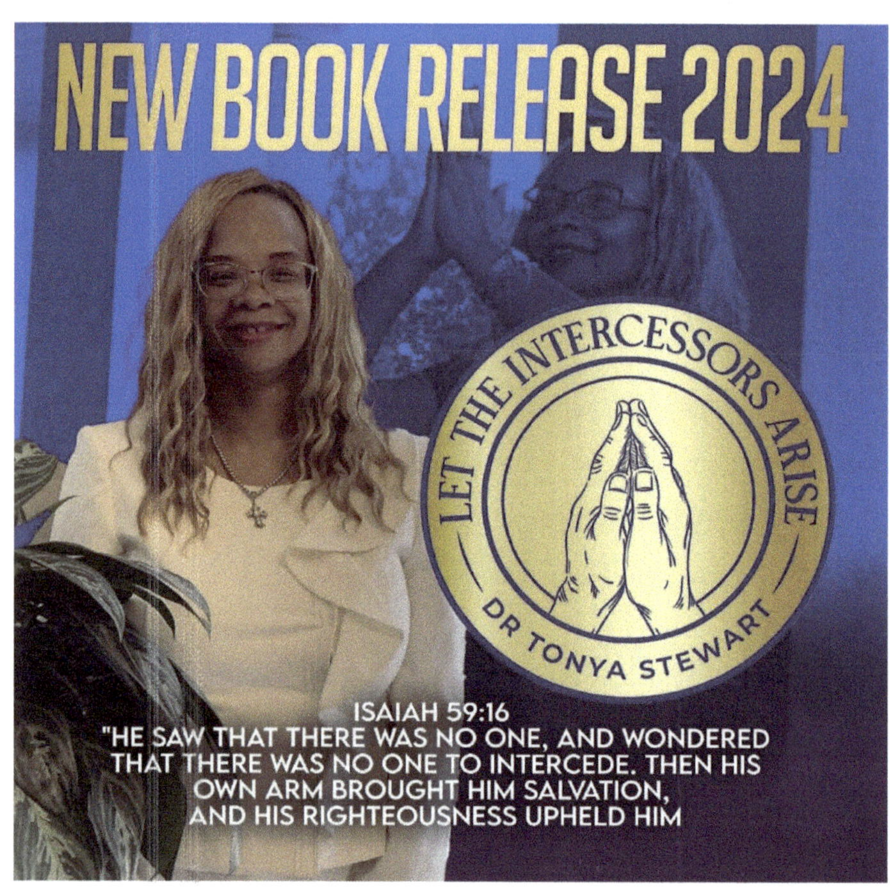

NEW BOOK RELEASE 2024
LET THE INTERCESSORS ARISE
DR TONYA STEWART
ISAIAH 59:16
"HE SAW THAT THERE WAS NO ONE, AND WONDERED
THAT THERE WAS NO ONE TO INTERCEDE. THEN HIS
OWN ARM BROUGHT HIM SALVATION,
AND HIS RIGHTEOUSNESS UPHELD HIM

www.ingramcontent.com/pod-product-compliance
Lightning Source LLC
Chambersburg PA
CBHW050016040726
47599CB00014B/1402